# Chinese Proverbs

## 中國成語

Library of Congress Cataloging-in-Publication Data available.

ISBN 0-8118-3683-5

Manufactured in Hong Kong

Designed by Chen Design Associates

Distributed in Canada by Raincoast Books
9050 Shaughnessy Street
Vancouver, British Columbia V6P 6E5

10 9 8 7 6 5 4 3 2 1

Chronicle Books LLC
85 Second Street
San Francisco, California 94105

www.chroniclebooks.com

# Chinese Proverbs

## 中國成語

*Collected by* Ruthanne Lum McCunn

*Introduction by* K. L. Kiu

*Illustrations by* Hu Yong Yi

**CHRONICLE BOOKS**

SAN FRANCISCO

Proverbs, wise sayings rooted in familiar experience, open a window to the life and customs of a nation and a people. In this delightful collection of traditional Chinese proverbs we are offered a fascinating glimpse into the long-ago daily lives of the Chinese people.

Farming has been the main occupation in China for many centuries and we see this in proverbs such as "You cannot help shoots grow by pulling them up" and "Sow melon, reap melon; sow beans, reap beans." Raising livestock has also provided insights ("As a pig fears getting fat, so a man fears renown"). To the Chinese, eating and drinking have always been of primary importance and truths stated through food and drink especially hit home: "The eyes are wide but the stomach is narrow" is directed at impractical people, while we find a lament over good friends who must inevitably part rendered as "On earth no feast lasts forever." Shrewd business sense is revealed in

"A person without a smiling face should not open
a shop" and the concern for appearances prompts
"A lean dog shames its master." Popular pastimes
such as chess and hunting, too, have contributed
to the rich treasury of life in these aphorisms, as we
see in "Observers can see a chess game more clearly
than the players" and "When the rabbits are dead,
the hounds that tracked them will be cooked."

The proverbs themselves are drawn from sources as
diverse as literary classics, political slogans, and folk
wisdom passed on from parents to children. "Do not
climb a tree to look for fish," for example, is adapted
from the advice of the famous fourth-century B.C.
Chinese philosopher Mencius, who held that "Seeking
the fulfilment of such an ambition by such means as
you employ is like looking for fish by climbing a tree"
(from *Mencius*, translated by D. C. Lau). One of the most
well-known sayings of Deng Xiaoping, bearing his

pragmatism as a leader of the modern Chinese nation, has entered the language as the proverb "It does not matter if the cat is black or white so long as it catches rats." The down-to-earth advice "If the horse dies, then you have to walk" probably originated in folk wisdom, as two of the three verbs in the original Chinese are found in the oral form of the Cantonese dialect.

Proverbs may contain profound truths, but their meanings must be presented clearly if their true color and significance is to be conveyed. Ruthanne Lum McCunn, who collected and provided the English renditions of these proverbs, has succeeded admirably in preserving these important qualities, and readers of this book will have no need of footnotes or explanations to enjoy these wise sayings handed down by generations of Chinese people.

K. L. Kiu

An old horse
knows the way.

老馬識途

縁
木
求
魚

Do not
climb a tree
to look for fish.

眼闊肚窄

The eyes are
wide but the
stomach is
narrow.

As a pig fears
getting fat,
so a man
fears renown.

人怕出名豬怕壯。

Water
can
drip
through
stone.

水滴石穿

鼠有鼠道

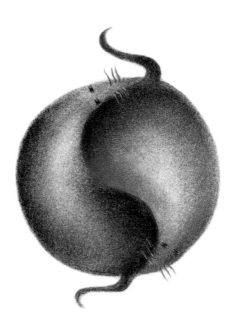

Rats know
the way of rats.

狗瘦主人羞。

A lean dog
shames
its master.

The cunning hare
has three burrows.

狡兔三窟

下雨擋風　才是好朋友。

A good friend
shields you
from the storm.

明槍易躲，
　　暗箭難防。

It is easy to dodge a spear
you can see,

difficult to guard against an arrow
shot from hiding.

20

虎鹿不同行。

Tigers and deer
do not walk together.

臨淵羨魚，不如退而結網。

Better to make a net
than to yearn for fish
at the edge of a pond.

Ants can move
even a mighty mountain.

螞 蟻 能 搬 山 。

窮 鼠 齧 貓

A cornered rat will bite the cat.

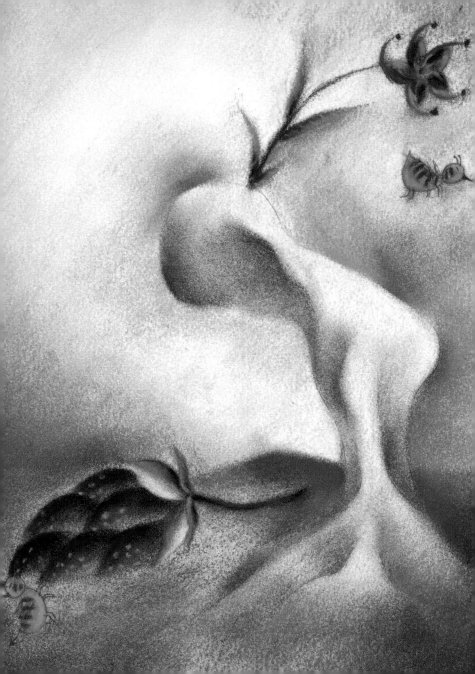

A good bee
never takes pollen
from a fallen flower.

落地花。

好蜂不採

當局者迷，
　旁觀者清。

Observers
can see
a chess game
more clearly
than the players.

畫餅充飢

You cannot satisfy hunger
by drawing a cake.

Serving
the powerful
is like
sleeping
with a tiger.

伴君如伴虎。

眞金不怕火煉。

Genuine gold
fears no fire.

Crows are black
the world over.

天下烏鴉一般黑。

32

種瓜得瓜，種豆得豆。

Sow melon,
reap melon;
sow beans,
reap beans.

飲水思源

When you drink water,
remember the source.

Rivers and mountains are
more easily changed than a
man's nature.

江山易改，

　　本性難移。

A person without a smiling face
should not open a shop.

人無笑臉

　　不開店。

星星之火，可以燎原。

A single spark
can set a prairie
on fire.

狗兔死，走狗烹。

When the rabbits
are dead,
the hounds that
tracked them
will be cooked.

拔苗助長

You cannot
help shoots grow
by pulling them up.

樹倒猢猻散。

When a tree falls,
the monkeys scatter.

A mouse can see only an inch.

鼠目寸光

盡信書不如無書。

Better to do
without books
than to believe
everything they say.

騎
虎
難
下

It is difficult to get off a tiger's back.

A swallow
cannot know
the lofty ambitions
of an eagle.

燕雀豈知　鴻鵠之志。

良藥苦口

Good medicine
is bitter to the taste.

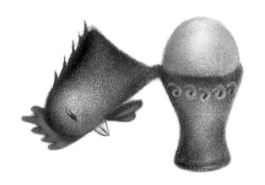

# 殺雞取卵

Do not kill
the hen
for her eggs.

Water can both sustain
and sink a ship.

水能載舟，也能覆舟。

不入虎穴，焉得虎子。

If you do not brave the tiger's lair,
how can you capture the cub?

You cannot clap
with one hand.

孤掌難鳴

聚
蚊
成
雷

A swarm of mosquitoes
can sound like thunder.

On earth
no feast
lasts forever.

天下無不散之筵席。

各花入各眼。

Flowers look  different
to different eyes.

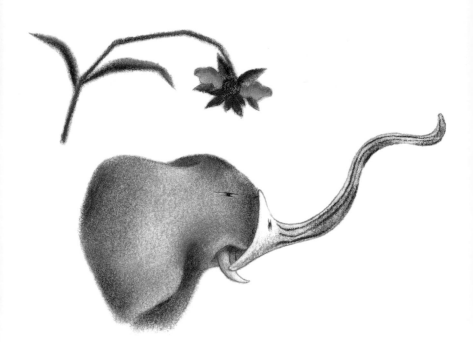

人心不足蛇吞象。

An avaricious person
is like a snake
trying to swallow
an elephant.

覆
水
難
收

Spilt water
cannot be
retrieved.

殺雞焉用牛刀

You do not need
a butcher's knife
to kill a chicken.

木本水源

A tree has its roots,
a stream its source.

臨渴掘井

Do not wait
until you're thirsty
to dig a well.

人靠衣裳　馬靠鞍。

A man is judged by his clothes,
a horse by its saddle.

Trees may prefer calm,
but the wind will not subside.

樹欲靜而風不止。

一腳不踏二船。

One foot
cannot stand
on two boats.

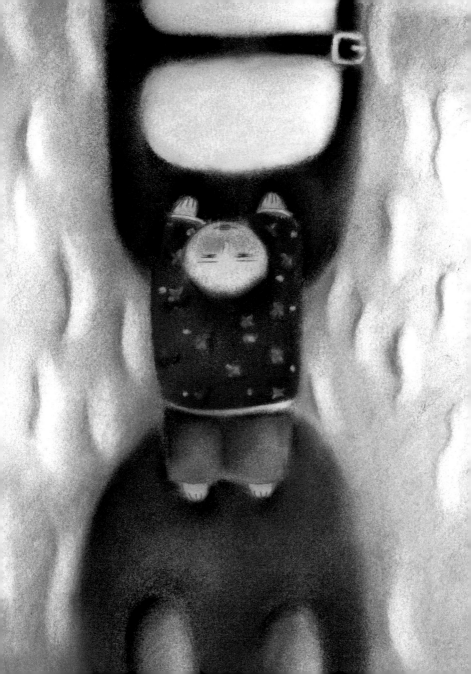

麻雀雖小，五臟俱全。

The sparrow may be small
but it has all the vital organs.

When weeding,
destroy the roots.

斬草除根

Better to be
a rooster's beak
than a bull's rump.

寧爲雞口，勿爲牛後。

# 狗嘴裡吐
## 不出象牙。

Ivory does not come out
of a dog's mouth.

When you paint a dragon,
dot its eyes.

畫龍點睛

不管黑貓白貓，抓到老鼠就是好貓。

It does not matter
if the cat is black or white
so long as it catches rats.

馬死落地行。

If the horse dies,
then you have to walk.

If you do not climb
the mountain,
you will not see
the plain.

不上高山，
不顯平地。

佛口蛇心

Beware the person
with a Buddha's mouth
and a snake's heart.

路遙知馬力，

日久見人心。

Distance tests the
endurance of a horse;
time reveals
a man's character.